o(n.k)   M
W £2-00

This book is to be returne
the last date stamped

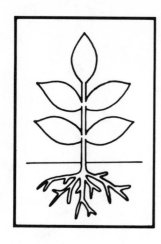

CHEMISTRY
CAREERS

by L. B. Taylor, Jr.

CHEMISTRY
CAREERS

FRANKLIN WATTS | NEW YORK | LONDON | 1978

Photographs courtesy of: Eastman Kodak Company: pp. 2, 10; Union Carbide Corporation: pp. 19 (top), 41; Dow Chemical U.S.A.: pp. 19 (bottom), 26, 30, 35 (top), 47; The DuPont Company: pp. 22, 54; Pfizer, Inc.: p. 35 (bottom); The Shell Companies: p. 36.

Library of Congress Cataloging in Publication Data

Taylor, L   B
    Chemistry careers.

    (A Career concise guide)
    Bibliography: p.
    Includes index.
    SUMMARY: Discusses chemistry jobs in industries, institutions, schools, and government, their educational requirements, and salary ranges.
    1. Chemical engineering—Vocational guidance—Juvenile literature. 2. Chemistry—Vocational guidance—Juvenile literature. [1. Chemistry—Vocational guidance. 2. Chemical engineering—Vocational guidance. 3. Vocational guidance] I. Title.
TP186.T38   540'.23   77–21313
ISBN 0–531–01420–7

D
540·23
TAY

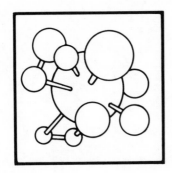

Contents

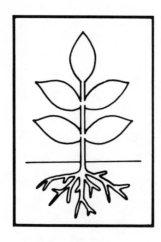

CHEMISTRY
CAREERS

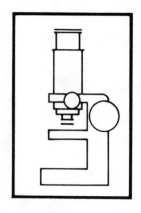

Why Chemistry?

Chemicals, in one form or another, are involved in just about everything around us. The air we breathe is chemical. So, too, is the food we eat, the water we drink, and much of the materials and energy sources we use to build and heat our homes. Even our own bodies and the life processes that sustain them are chemical in nature. The food we eat undergoes many chemical changes in our bodies.

Products of chemical research, development, and production surround us daily. Consider as examples, the dishes on which we eat, the asphalt on which we ride, and the paper on which we write. Take the color of carpets, photos in albums, radios, and tapes and phonograph records. Or think about transistors and telephones, bathtubs and boats, raincoats and soaps, toothpastes, perfumes, and deodorants. All of these, and countless other products, are chemical in nature, or used chemistry at some point in their development.

How fully does chemistry affect our lives? In the food industry, for instance, processors use chemical knowledge of the basic structure of foods—proteins, carbohydrates, fats, vitamins, and minerals—to produce better, healthier foods. Chemical fertilizers greatly increase farm production. Pesticides, insecticides and fun-

**This research chemist is working on
new photographic color-forming techniques.**

gicides, developed in chemical laboratories, protect food harvests from the ravages of insects, weeds, and diseases. And the contents of our market baskets are not only healthier, but more attractive, fresher, and available the year round because of chemistry.

Look at how chemistry has helped revolutionize the health and medical field. Through the miracles of pharmaceuticals, we have defeated such dread diseases as diptheria, typhoid, whooping cough, and polio, among others. And we have produced pain relievers and infection fighters ranging from everyday aspirin to penicillin.

In the textile industry, synthetic fibers such as nylon, polyester, and acrylics have become predominant in our clothing. These same chemically produced fibers make up most of our carpets, rugs, and drapes. Such materials wear better, last longer, are maintained more easily, and can be made in a greater variety of colors and styles than ever before.

The housing and construction industries use asphalt for roofs, plastic for piping and gypsum, chemically treated paper for wallboard, and a broad range of better quality paints. The electronics industry uses the techniques of chemical purification and crystallization, among others, to produce transistors, portable television sets, hearing aids and heart pacemakers, and a vast range of large and small appliances to better our lives.

Nuclear energy, too, relies on chemistry and chemical engineering. The manufacture of iron and steel is a chemical process. And chemists and chemical engineers helped develop most of the processes used in petroleum refining.

These are only a few representative examples of how chemistry and chemical products touch almost every facet of our lives.

[3]

CHEMICAL PEOPLE

People in the chemical industry today find excitement in learning about nature, and they realize a sense of personal fulfillment in helping to provide products and services needed by others.

But people who choose careers in this broad field are not satisfied with past accomplishments. They are working today on finding solutions to such crucial problem areas as the environment, energy, and health. And they are continually searching for the technical breakthroughs that will lead to better products for tomorrow.

Chemists and chemical engineers have a broad range of career fields to select from. Some choose service with the U.S. Government, which uses many chemical professionals in such agencies as the Department of Agriculture, the Department of Health, Education and Welfare, and the Energy Research and Development Agency, for example.

Others, especially those interested in research, may seek employment with nationally famous institutes, such as Battelle Memorial Laboratories or the Stanford Research Institute.

There are many careers open to the chemistry graduate interested in teaching—from junior high school through the nation's leading colleges and universities. A great deal of basic research work is carried out in academic institutions, too.

The greatest number of job opportunities, and the widest range of positions, is available through companies in the chemical industry, which develop and manufacture products.

There are several major branches of chemistry to consider in choosing a career field. Among them:

—In organic chemistry, people study or work with

[4]

compounds that contain carbon, in combination with hydrogen and other nonmetals. Such compounds include not only those found in living organisms, but also those found in minerals and synthetic compounds.

—Inorganic chemists study or work with compounds that do not contain carbon. These include metals, radioactive elements, and the commercial acids, bases, and salts commonly used in the products of the chemical industry.

—Physical chemists study the physical characteristics of chemical substances, searching for answers in precise mathematical terms that explain the structure of atoms and molecules, and the mechanism of chemical reactions.

—Biochemists often work in agriculture or medicine. They are concerned with the compounds present in living organisms; how they are formed from simple materials and how they are broken down by living cells.

—Analytical chemists use sophisticated instruments and other techniques to probe the identity of chemical substances, and estimate the quantities present.

—Chemical engineers are responsible for the production of chemical substances and the control of chemical processes in laboratories and plants.

There are hundreds of specialized job possibilities branching out from these main sections.

Many positions in the chemical career field require college degrees. Some highly specialized jobs demand advanced degrees—a master's or Ph.D. However, there are also many positions open to high school graduates and to those who have had some college training, or have studied in night school or through correspondence courses. These people might work as chemical technologists, laboratory technicians, or production workers.

Chemical careers offer excellent challenges and opportunities because the chemical industry is a growth field with an ever-present need for qualified young men and women. It is an interesting and exciting career area, it pays well, and it offers the opportunity for advancement.

In short, a chemical career offers opportunity for self-fulfillment, whether your objective is service, responsibility, professional recognition, monetary reward, or any combination of these.

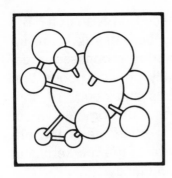

The Thrill of Discovery

A common definition of research is, "the use of systematic methods to evaluate ideas or to discover new knowledge." One of America's most famous inventive geniuses, Charles F. Kettering, said, "research is nothing but a state of mind—a friendly, welcoming attitude toward change, going out to look for change instead of waiting for it to come. The research state of mind is the problem-solving mind as contrasted to the let-well-enough-alone mind. It is the 'tomorrow' mind instead of the 'yesterday' mind."

Researchers in chemistry and in other career fields are the free-thinkers, the dreamers. They have long-sighted vision that searches beyond day-to-day problems and obstacles for better, more imaginative, more creative ways of doing things. Innovation and ideas are as much a part of their "tools of trade" as are microscopes and calculators.

Research is the vital lifeblood of the chemical industry. In fact, the industry spends a higher percentage of its money for research, and employs twice as many research experts, as any other career field.

Most companies, of all sizes, maintain research laboratories or support research conducted by other organizations. These efforts result in development of thousands of new products and processes.

Why is so much emphasis placed on research? Because competition in the chemical business is keen. Ingenuity in products and manufacturing processes is essential for a company to continually provide goods that will satisfy the ever-changing wants and needs of consumers. And it is these fresh ideas that originate in research and development work that often mean the difference between success and failure in the marketplace; between growth and progress, or stagnancy.

There are two primary kinds of research careers in chemistry. One is basic, or fundamental, research. The other is applied research, which offers a far greater number of job opportunities.

BASIC RESEARCH

In basic research, chemists try to learn more about nature in general. Through experiments and study programs in government, university, institutional, and industrial laboratories, they seek to broaden the horizons of knowledge. They explore the unknown, often obtaining results that are both unpredictable and unexpected.

Some projects may take months or even years to complete, or may never get completed. Yet always there is the excitement of knowing that from basic research comes discoveries that change our lives for the better.

Although there are many disappointments and frustrations in basic research, there are also major discoveries and technological breakthroughs—in medicine, agriculture, textiles, petroleum, and scores of other fields. For example, the discovery of nylon and other polymers and plastics resulted from fundamental studies of large molecules by chemists in industrial laboratories.

APPLIED RESEARCH

More down-to-earth is applied research. This is where physical applications of chemistry to consumer goods and services are sought. Applied research tries to improve chemical products and processes, or develop new ones. Basic knowledge is directed toward a specific product.

By far the largest career field in applied research is industrial chemistry, involving the production of raw materials and the development of industrial chemical products. For example, research efforts in agriculture have led to such new chemicals as insecticide sprays that protect crops. Other chemicals today help speed plant growth. Applied research in the biological sciences and medicine has led to a number of new drugs that fight disease and infection. In fact, pharmaceutical companies sometimes spend from one-third to one-half of their earnings on research leading to new medical products.

In the physical sciences, chemical studies of the properties of matter lead to the discovery of new or improved metals. In the petroleum industry, researchers constantly seek new and better ways to extract oil and gas from the earth, and develop methods of improving such everyday products as gasoline for more efficient use.

Researchers also look for ways to upgrade present chemical manufacturing processes and machinery, and to reduce costs of production while keeping quality high.

The day of unrestrained pollution of our natural environment is gone. The chemical industry recognizes that it must dispose of its wastes in a way that will protect the natural environment.

Thus, one of the fastest growing research career

areas in chemistry is in the environmental/ecological field. Some chemical products are derived from toxic substances and are potentially dangerous. Other chemicals are potentially harmful to the atmosphere and to waterways as pollutants.

So much attention today is being focused on research and development of safe, efficient ways to handle such materials so that they are not harmful to people or to the environment. This includes working in imaginative ways to control and reduce noise, fumes, odors, and exposure to hazardous materials. In some cases, such studies lead to new and better products. As one example, bio-degradable detergents were developed because of the pollution caused by normal detergents. New, more effective insecticides, without harmful side effects to the environment, also were discovered through research efforts.

Additionally, many researchers today are working on more efficient ways to use the great amounts of energy needed in the manufacture and production of chemicals. Many of these chemicals and the means of producing them are petroleum-based, and petroleum is becoming scarcer and more expensive. So such studies are very important. For instance, some waste products once released into the atmosphere, often as pollutants, are now being recycled as heat energy.

PERSONAL QUALITIES

To pursue a career in chemical research, you should first have a high degree of curiosity, creativity, and imagina-

A chemist developing methods for measuring impurities in materials.

tion. This should include the ability to depart from standard methods, if necessary, to solve a problem. For above all, the successful researcher must be able to develop and try new ideas.

Patience, too, is important, because researchers often must make many attempts at solving a problem before they are successful. Further, a chemical researcher should have the ability to communicate ideas effectively. He or she must be able to show what a particular project will mean to the company, agency, or research organization in order to obtain financial support for the program.

Perhaps the most important qualities in a chemical researcher are analytical ability and inventiveness. Recognizing opportunity for new ideas, and bringing them into reality are the researcher's main responsibilities. He or she must be able to find creative solutions to real problems . . . to devise ways to improve quality, reduce costs, or increase efficiency.

Besides being an expert in his or her field, the researcher must be flexible enough to see a project through from the initial idea to installation in a manufacturing plant.

RESEARCH OPPORTUNITIES

While most research careers in chemistry are with industrial companies, there are also many opportunities with government and independent research institutions. Research in colleges and universities will be discussed separately.

U.S. Government research organizations, for example, include the Public Health Service, and the regional laboratories of the Department of Agriculture, as well as the newer environmental and energy agencies. Independent research institutions serve industry, government, and private organizations on a contract basis.

For most professional positions in chemical research, a college degree in chemistry or chemical engineering is required. Most research department leaders in industry, and most chemists working in basic research, especially in universities and institutions, have advanced degrees, most often Ph.D.s.

Some companies staff a large number of their permanent research positions with holders of advanced degrees, then assign management trainees with B.S. degrees to temporary positions in the research department. These new employees work closely with experienced researchers.

However, there are many careers in chemical research laboratories open to the noncollege graduate. One way to enter these careers—a way that is becoming increasingly popular—is through training in chemical technology. Many schools, particularly junior and community colleges, today offer a two-year "associate degree" program in chemical technology. Study emphasis is on chemistry, physics, and mathematics, with special courses on instrumentation, electronics, industrial measurement, quantitative analysis, technical communications, and principles of automatic control, among others.

High school graduates are also hired as laboratory assistants and are sometimes given substantial responsibility. In some cases their work schedules are arranged to allow them to go to college while employed. High school graduates who show an aptitude for research work usually begin as laboratory trainees. Often they rotate jobs after six months or so, to gain a broader background and familiarity with various equipment, techniques, and problems.

Through on-the-job training or night school, lab

[13]

trainees may advance to higher positions, such as laboratory technicians, research technicians, and senior research technicians.

Beyond this, advancement can be made to the position of technologist in larger companies. These positions are usually open to those who have a combination of school study, studies at home or by correspondence school, and in-depth work experience equivalent to a B.S. technical degree. Technologists must show the ability to work independently with initiative and innovativeness, and be able to plan and carry out projects in a fully professional manner.

REWARDS IN RESEARCH

What rewards does a career in research bring? First, in chemistry, salaries are equal to or better than research salaries in other industries.

But pay is only one measure of reward. Chemical research programs are among the most progressive in any industry. The environment is stimulating and the researcher has access to the latest in scientific equipment. He or she can keep abreast of current developments in scientific knowledge through the excellent technical libraries maintained by companies, institutions, universities, and government agencies.

Research is also the career starting point for many young chemists. It provides an excellent background for advancement into other areas of chemical activity, such as manufacturing, management, or marketing. Many top managers of leading chemical companies began their careers in research. In fact, a large number of companies start new chemists and chemical engineers in research, on assignments lasting up to two years, and then transfer them to advanced positions in other areas.

Perhaps the most important reward of a career in research is personal satisfaction—the excitement of solving complex problems with creative ideas, the pride in creating something new and being recognized for it.

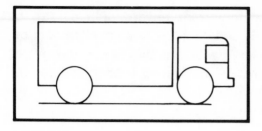

Pilot
Plants

The bridge between research and the production line in chemical companies is called development. This is the domain of the chemical engineer and the commercial development chemist. These people take the products and processes conceived in the laboratories and carry them through the successive stages of field evaluation, pilot plant design and tryout, and plant design and construction. They end up with a working manufacturing operation that is safe, ecologically sound, efficient, and economical.

CHEMICAL DEVELOPMENT
AND PROCESS ENGINEERS

A career in chemical development requires close cooperation with other professionals and technicians. For example, the development engineer must work with the researchers who performed the basic laboratory work. They must also team with pipe fitters, electricians, boilermakers, mechanics, and other skilled craftspeople who build pilot plant facilities. Pilot plants are smaller versions of actual production plants, where the manufacturing process, or the making of a new product, can be tested on a relatively small scale.

This is necessary because sometimes the concepts generated in the research laboratories, which work admirably on a small scale, do not always measure up under actual operating conditions. And since the cost of building new chemical plants and facilities is so excessively high, it is important to make sure any new product or process is practical before committing millions of dollars to it.

Once the pilot plant has been built, the commercial development chemist or chemical engineer must carefully monitor its operation, using a variety of sophisticated equipment, including computers, to gather the data necessary to justify further development.

If the product or process checks out at this level, the next step is to gear up for full production. Here, the development experts work closely with chemical process engineers. They must take the laboratory information and the pilot plant data and scale it up to full-size plant operations.

These chemists and chemical engineers must ask and find answers to such questions as: What size equipment will be needed? How much water, steam, and electricity would be used? How much would the new facilities cost to build? How much would it cost to produce the product by this new process?

Using all data available, these engineers next establish the heat and material requirements, and write up process "flowsheets," which are like charts that follow the process step by step. With the assistance of draftspersons and computers, the engineers translate these flowsheets into piping and instrument diagrams, identifying the size of equipment and the materials of construction to be used.

Process engineers must also work with many other professionals and specialists, so that their end product is a process that will operate safely and economically, and stand up under all conditions.

Once the design project is completed, however, the

process engineers do not lose sight of it. They work with mechanical, civil, and electrical engineering and construction people, acting as advisors in areas relating to the process. They tackle problems that may arise during the construction phase.

Finally, they are on hand for the starting of the process, when their design—which is on a scale of anywhere from ten to a thousand times larger than the pilot plant stage—results in an operating plant.

Additionally, much of the chemical process engineer's work is devoted to improving or expanding existing processes for major products. The use of new ideas and the effective streamlining of processes is very important to keep chemical products competitive in the marketplace.

In a sense, the work of chemical development and process engineers is never completed. Their task is a continual quest to improve product quality, increase production yield, reduce cost, and improve safety conditions. Much of this work is done in cooperation with chemists, instrumentation engineers, and production specialists.

CAREER OR STEPPING-STONE

Chemical engineers in either development or process engineering can make their work a lifelong career, or they can move into other fields, or up the management ladder. Many move into production work. Others use their

Above: a chemical engineer reviews the design of a pilot plant. Below: this chemical engineer is instructing a production worker in the operation of the pilot plant.

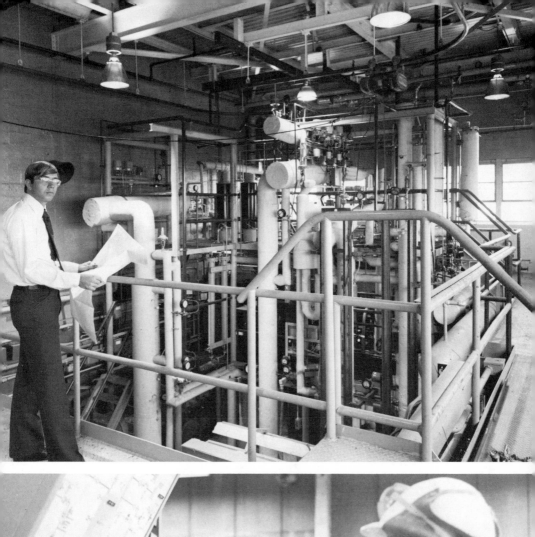

overall knowledge spanning research and production, and their ability to work well with people in many disciplines, to become supervisors, superintendents, or managers of plants or specific chemical departments. Thus, careers in development and process engineering are excellent all-around training grounds for chemical engineers with leadership qualities.

A degree in chemical engineering is essential to become a development or processing engineer. However, many assistants and technicians in a broad range of fields are needed to help build, analyze, and evaluate pilot plant and production plant start-ups and operations. And many chemists become involved in one or more aspects of the commercial development process.

Studies in engineering, basic chemistry, drafting, construction, and computer operations are helpful for these kinds of jobs.

Pay scales for chemical engineers are higher than for most other engineering fields. Salaries may start at $12,000 a year or more for those with B.S. degrees. Also, the demand for chemical engineers is high and the supply is often short. Pay for technicians and others assisting chemical engineers is also good.

But to many who choose this career area, a more satisfying reward is the sense of accomplishment they receive from transforming research data and blueprints into active, multimillion-dollar chemical buildings and busy production lines turning out products for improved living.

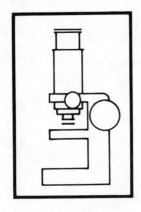

On The Firing Line

In the chemical industry, the production plant is the action center. Here is where all the elements come together, where ideas tested in the laboratories and pilot plants are put to work. Production people use raw materials, heat, and power to manufacture the products that have been spawned in research, nurtured through development, and will be marketed and sold to consumers all over the world.

It is a constant, day-to-day challenge to chemical engineers and chemists in production to turn out the most products, of the highest quality, in the safest manner, for the lowest possible cost. How well and consistently these goals are met often makes the difference between the success and failure of a product in the marketplace.

Generally, overall responsibility for running a chemical plant belongs to the production engineers. The job is a real test of his or her leadership and human relations skills because these people are accountable for the productivity, safety, and morale of employees.

The chemical production engineer works with:

—People in the purchasing department (who obtain raw materials).

—Utility companies (for electricity and steam).

—Maintenance services (to keep plant equipment in good working order).

—Marketing personnel (to coordinate production schedules with customer needs).

—Product development and customer service people (on product specifications and customer needs).

—Research and process department specialists (on new projects to improve production).

—Process engineers (to streamline current processes).

Production engineers find their work fast-moving and challenging, requiring them to think intelligently and act quickly in analyzing unexpected problems. Some of the problems they could encounter include: raw material shortages, or variations in its quality; labor disruptions; increasing costs; equipment breakdowns; and adverse weather conditions. In each instance, the engineer, with help from staff members, must think through the problem and arrive at the best, quickest, safest solution. In most cases this means keeping the plant running at all times. A plant shutdown can mean excessive losses in time and money.

CHEMISTS IN PRODUCTION

Many chemists also find production a satisfying career field. Many large chemical manufacturing units maintain their own quality control laboratories, requiring the services of chemists for analytical work. They use modern,

Chemical engineers must work together in developing an efficient production system.

sophisticated equipment to make sure the chemicals being processed are of a consistent high quality.

Other chemists are employed as "troubleshooters" who try to get more out of the manufacturing process, or work on new building projects. These include equipment replacements and new facilities, and the size and scope of such a project can range from the simple replacement of a pump in an existing plant, to the design, construction, and start-up of a whole new complex.

In many instances, the lines of distinction between chemists and chemical engineers in production plants become virtually invisible. So often chemists can be found in just about every type of manufacturing job category.

While a degree in chemistry or chemical engineering is essential for most management and upper supervisory positions in production, there are many other attractive careers open for the high school graduate.

PRODUCTION TECHNICIANS

Trained technicians and operators run much of the equipment and machinery used in the manufacture of chemical products. Such equipment is very complicated and must be handled with a high degree of skill. The people in these jobs have a lot of responsibility and a lot of independence. Often they operate this equipment with little or no direct supervision. They perform daily checks on the quality and quantity of the products at each step of the production process. Technicians also operate the control rooms, maintaining a constant watch on temperatures, pressures, and various other factors important in chemical processing.

Technicians must keep complex equipment and machines in good, safe working order, and be able to help diagnose problems in virtually every type of equipment and facility in the plant. Additionally, chemical plants usually incorporate a variety of heating, airconditioning, electrical, materials handling, environmental control, and other systems—all of which must be operated and maintained by plant engineers and technicians.

A good mechanical aptitude and vocational technical training are desirable for technician and operator jobs in chemical manufacturing. Salaries for these production workers, according to a 1975 Department of Labor study, average from 55¢ to $1.10 an hour higher than the average paid to workers in general manufacturing. Production people in the chemical end of the petroleum and coal industries average even more.

Chemical engineers and chemists who do well in production are in an excellent position to advance rapidly, since chemical companies' growth in facilities is constantly creating new positions of greater responsibility. Production engineers can become senior production engineers, plant superintendents, section managers, production managers, plant managers, and division general managers. Many company presidents and other top executives started out or advanced their careers in production work, gaining invaluable experience and knowledge.

In addition to a degree in chemical engineering or chemistry, prospective production engineers should have leadership qualities and must be able to work well with people. They should possess the ability to lead people to more productive work.

The rewards for such a person are excellent. Starting salaries for professional production people in the chemical industry are considerably higher than those

**Manufacturing plant superintendents are responsible
for shipping, in addition to many other duties.**

in most other competitive fields, and are comparable to those in product development or process engineering—about $12,000 a year or more for those with a B.S. degree.

But there are other satisfying rewards for those who choose a career in chemical production. You are given a large amount of responsibility almost immediately; more so than in any other career area of chemistry. You are on the manufacturing firing line, where the action is, every day. And your chance for advancement and promotion is limited only by your own talents, ideas, and initiative.

MAINTENANCE AND UTILITIES

Related career fields in chemical production for those who do not attend college include maintenance and utilities. Maintenance is a job that appeals to people with a mechanical aptitude and some knowledge or experience in such areas as wiring, plumbing, carpentry, and others.

Maintenance specialists help keep chemical plants operating at maximum efficiency. They assist engineers in installing new equipment and keeping other equipment in good working condition. They maintain buildings and grounds. Advantages of this type of job include working outside some of the time, and an endless variety of assignments—from stocking and operating parts warehouses, to performing minor construction and equipment repairs.

Utilities personnel get involved with environmental control efforts, such as water cleaning projects, operating steam generators and boilers, and taking care of waste disposal.

Jobs in maintenance and utilities generally are open to high school graduates, with most training done on the job. These entry-level positions often can lead to jobs in chemical production or as laboratory assistants.

Pay is a little higher than similar jobs in other industries, and most maintenance and utilities people in chemicals work a straight forty-hour week.

INDUSTRIAL SERVICE

An interesting career field that is a direct offshoot of the chemical production business, and one that does not necessarily require college training, is industrial service.

It is the job of these engineers and technicians to chemically remove and prevent efficiency-robbing deposits in industrial process equipment. Customers for such services form a broad cross section that includes utilities, refineries, and manufacturers of steel, paper, chemical, and petrochemicals, among others.

Industrial service specialists do their work in the field. They use pipe wrenches as well as calculators, and they are as comfortable in a pair of coveralls as they are in business suits.

Each assignment is different in this fast-growing profession. One week the task may call for the cleaning of a utility company's water lines containing heavy deposits of debris. Another may require the removal of metallic deposits at a plant site through the use of special chemical agents.

The job is far more than just "getting one's hands dirty." Expensive, complex technical equipment is used to help make plants and equipment worth millions of dollars cleaner and more efficient to operate.

Industrial service is an area where creativity and innovation are valuable assets. Each job tests the engineer's "troubleshooting" analytical abilities as to how to perform it safely and effectively.

The rewards include good pay, travel, a wide variety

of challenging assignments, and the satisfaction of deciding on your own how best to carry them out.

Industrial service engineers should have a college degree in chemical, mechanical, or industrial engineering. Technicians should have at least a high school education and an aptitude for working with equipment.

DISTRIBUTION AND TRAFFIC

A specialized career of vital importance in the chemical industry is distribution and traffic. Many customers who use chemical products have plants and factories that are hundreds, even thousands of miles away from the site where they are manufactured. Also, since many chemicals are highly volatile and potentially hazardous, they must be handled and transported with special care.

Thus, getting the right product to the right place at the right time, on a global scale, is a challenging profession in itself that extends far beyond routine freight rates, transportation schedules, and zip codes. Distribution and traffic is the principal link between manufacturing and marketing.

With many chemical companies, distribution involves helping to establish market and manufacturing requirements, reviewing sales estimates, controlling inventories, and developing internal and outside distribution systems. Estimators and planners develop short- and long-term sales estimates, schedule production requirements, maintain inventories, and study business forecasts.

People in traffic operations work closely with experts in the transportation industry. Most chemicals and chemical products are shipped by truck, specialized vans, railroad tank cars, and by ships—everything from

barges to supertankers. The on-time, safe dispatching and delivery of enormous shipments is a complex, demanding job.

Distribution and traffic specialists make ample use of computers in their work. Order processing, inventory accounting, billing for exports, transportation planning and scheduling—all are functions that are computer controlled in most instances.

Companies prefer people in this field with degrees in industrial distribution, traffic, logistics, mathematics, economics, accounting, business administration, industrial management, computer science, or liberal arts. However, high school graduates may start out as clerks, computer operators, or administrative assistants, and work their way up through on-the-job training and experience.

While the pay is not usually as high as with chemists or chemical engineers in research, development, or production, it is above the average of other industries.

This product manager must see that supplies are always available to the plant.

[31]

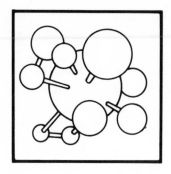

Satisfaction in Sales

One of the most interesting, challenging, and satisfying jobs in the industry—with rewards commensurate with abilities and determination—is that of the chemical salesperson.

People in chemical sales are bound only by the limits of their individual initiative, imagination, and innovation. To the more enterprising, a sales job can be a doorway to higher positions in marketing, general management, even the presidency or chairmanship of a company. Many top managers and chief executives in chemical companies today began or advanced their careers by working in sales.

Further, there is the personal satisfaction, to the salesperson, of knowing he or she is matching company products and services with important economic and social needs. Such products help control or abate water and air pollution, increase world food production, improve the safety and performance of automobiles, better the efficiency of energy uses, lengthen human life and improve human health, and many other things.

SALES OPPORTUNITIES

A chemical company is a place where products and services are developed to meet a great variety of human needs, and sales people have a primary role in this. They are the ones who see and understand the needs in the marketplace, and alert their research and product development specialists to those needs. Thus, they exert a strong influence on the company's direction.

Today, a salesperson can be a specialist or a jack-of-all-products, depending upon the size and scope of the employer. Small companies, for example, may manufacture only a few products and provide a limited number of services. Their sales staff generally must cover the range of this entire line.

With a large company, however, salespersons usually concentrate on one particular product line or service area. It could be, for example, agricultural products, or environmental control systems. The individual salesperson could specialize in solvents, or certain polymers, or oxides.

It is important for the new salesperson to first become thoroughly familiar with the products and services he or she has been assigned to. It is also important to know the customers and the competition. How can you better serve these customers? What are their special needs? What are the particular features of your products compared with those of your competitors?

In most cases, a new salesperson is assigned to a sales office, usually working with an experienced salesperson. Far from being routine, this job puts you in a spot where things are happening. You may have many contacts. You're the individual the customer turns to for shipping information, technical data, price quotations, or for help on any number of product and service subjects.

As an office salesperson, you use such tools as the telephone, teletype, and the business letter. The skillful use of these tools is important, because you are acting as the "bridge" between the company and the customer,

[33]

and vice versa. Salespeople work closely with such company service departments as scheduling and traffic, communications, sales adjustment, credit, and pricing, to name a few.

After gaining valuable experience in the office job, you then may move up to a field sales position. Here, the responsibility and the challenge increase. While you may report to a district sales manager, when you are calling on customers, *you* are the one in charge. You are the sole representative of your company and its products and services. You, at once, become salesperson, troubleshooter, public relations specialist, and citizen, all rolled into one.

You are, of course, backed up by everyone in your company, and no matter how far afield you are, they are no farther away than the telephone. Still, it is you who stirs them to action. And it is you who mainly symbolizes your company to customers, because you are the only person they see.

In field sales, you must become a veritable one-person intelligence agency and planning department. You are constantly on the alert for matchups between your products and customers' needs. And you must also look ahead, beyond today's sales, to the future.

You must ask, and seek answers to, what your customers will need tomorrow, and then get this information back to your company so newer, better, "second-generation" products can be developed. You must closely follow the research, not only of your company, but of your customers and your competitors as well.

Above: chemical field salesperson sets out for a sales call. Below: sales representatives maintain relations with many accounts and customers, and are always traveling.

Market researchers gather information on their products from dealers and retailers.

A sales position is not one for the timid or shy. There is a high degree of visibility to the job, and there is no place to hide. Much of your efforts are directly measurable. But to the outgoing person who loves a challenge and enjoys dealing with people, this is the ideal spot.

Requirements for a chemical salesperson vary from company to company. The one essential qualification is an ability to get along with people. You should be a good listener, and be able to understand what your customer wants. And you should be able to communicate this effectively to others in your company.

It is not absolutely essential, but it is a tremendous advantage to be well-grounded technically. Most large companies normally hire chemists and chemical engineers to fill their sales and marketing positions. Business-oriented and marketing courses of study are also recommended. If a person exhibits strong sales potential, however, technical training can be learned on the job.

A job in chemical sales can not only be a challenging and satisfying career in itself, but it also can prepare a person for a variety of related professional and management positions.

MARKET RESEARCH

Chemical market researchers work in the future. It is their job to study sales trends over the long-term, and advise their company's management what will be the products most in demand by customers over the next few years.

The more accurately they can forecast these projections, the better a company can meet future opportunities, improve its market position, and increase profits.

A college degree is needed for most of these positions, with emphasis on economics, statistics, marketing, and business administration. Some technical chemical knowledge is helpful. Market researchers also should be able to get along with people, because much of the information they need is obtained through exchanges with others in the industry, with consumers, retailers, distributors, and suppliers. They must keep a constant finger on the public's pulse, and develop the rare ability to project what the popular buying trends will be tomorrow in regard to chemical products.

Pay varies considerably, but generally is good, especially for those who enter the field with a master's degree in business administration plus a good background understanding of chemicals.

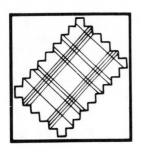

More Than Bunsen Burners

Several levels of jobs in teaching and consulting work are open to chemistry and chemical engineering students who complete their college studies and get degrees. In teaching alone, the positions range from junior high school to the university level, where professors guide graduate students through intricate and highly specialized research projects.

Many chemistry teachers begin their careers in secondary schools—junior high schools and high schools —where states have openings for such positions. Qualifications include at least a minor in chemistry studies, with a minimum of thirty college semester hours. Most public schools require a bachelor's degree, and some prefer a master's degree, so teachers may also instruct in such related fields as mathematics and physics.

Pay for teaching positions is considerably lower than for most jobs available in industry to college graduates—as much as $2,000 to $4,000 less. However, some young teachers start in secondary schools, continue their education while gaining experience, and advance to higher level teaching positions. Many also find great personal satisfaction in encouraging young people's interest in chemistry.

Also, some organizations, like the National Science Foundation, support teacher education and research.

During summers, one can attend intensive short courses, take regular courses, or work with an academic research scientist.

Another type of teaching is in technical institutes and junior colleges, and a master's degree in chemistry is usually required. As on the secondary school level, teaching in these schools and institutions covers a broad range of chemical subject matter, with relatively minor emphasis on research.

In small colleges and universities, instructors may become involved in some research work, but the emphasis is still mainly on teaching, and at this level a Ph.D. is often necessary.

RESEARCH PROGRAMS

It is in the larger colleges and the major universities where the lines between teaching and research work become blurred. Here, a Ph.D. is required, as well as postdoctoral studies in some cases.

At many of these schools, instructors and professors spend most of their time in research programs of their own, or directing research efforts of graduate students.

Most students have a rather clear idea of the role of the teacher. However, many students do not realize the degree of involvement of the university professor in guiding graduate students in research. Neither do they appreciate the impact that the professor's selection of research projects for students has on the student's career and upon government and industry. Both depend heavily on the technology developed at the university.

There are several reasons why colleges and universities actively seek research grants and programs from the U.S. Government, institutions, and private in-

**This research chemist is working
on developing a better adhesive.**

dustry. Such programs tend to attract good faculty members and students; they help pay expenses and salaries; they add prestige; and they generally upgrade the quality of the school.

Also, the subjects of research conducted at universities are often exciting. Many Nobel prize winners in chemistry received their awards while working on research projects in schools. A large degree of cancer research, for example, is conducted by teachers and professors on campuses, as well as various other programs ranging from agricultural projects to space programs to searches for more efficient energy sources.

Such research often is funded because government agencies or chemical companies cannot afford to maintain large staffs devoted to highly specialized work. Also, many faculty members, over the years, develop a level of expertise in a particular field of endeavor far advanced from that normally found outside of the academic area.

In fact, research programs in colleges and universities have become so important in recent years that many schools hire specialists to seek funds for such projects, and to manage research budgets and administration.

Those who direct research efforts in schools love their work. Because they have a light teaching load, they generally have a sizeable group of graduate assistants to help them, and they can concentrate on the specialized fields of their expertise.

In addition to the academic requirements, several years of experience are needed to reach this level. But the pay is good, the work is challenging and professionally satisfying, and the respect and honor accorded these career specialists is the highest in the chemical industry.

[42]

CONSULTANTS

A related career field involves consultants. These are people who have either a wide background of experience in general chemical management, or have developed expertise in a specialized field of chemistry.

Many college chemistry teachers or professors, for example, serve as consultants to industrial firms, usually on a part-time basis. They may be called in as "troubleshooters" to help solve a particular problem, or to give advice in an area in which they have specific knowledge. Or they may be asked to sit in on management meetings or become members of a company's board of directors.

Quite a few people, in fact, become full-time consultants to one or more companies or agencies, either working for themselves, or for a firm that sells consulting services to industry.

Pay for consultants varies greatly, depending on their degree of expertise, the number of companies they consult for, and the amount of time—part-time or full-time—their services are used. In all cases, however, the rate of pay, whether it is an hourly, monthly, or annual retainer, is excellent. Additionally, consultants are accorded honor and respect in recognition for their special knowledge.

Satellite Career Fields

INDUSTRIAL HYGIENE AND SAFETY

Industrial hygiene and safety engineers and technicians in the chemical industry have become more and more important in recent years, as more has been learned and reported about hazardous materials and their effects on employees working with them.

The handling of toxic substances, and the manufacture of such potentially harmful products as kepone and vinyl chloride have caused new laws and regulations to be written to safeguard plant workers and preserve the environment.

Industrial hygienists and safety specialists are charged with the responsibility for seeing that all environmental factors that might have some adverse effect on employees are carefully and safely controlled. Such factors may involve dusts, sprays, vapors, and aerosols or chemicals in the air.

The hygienists regularly inspect plants and laboratories, and use a variety of sophisticated scientific equipment to ensure that all employees are protected in safe working areas at all times.

For example, some chemicals used in water treatment and laboratories are strong enough to penetrate a person's skin. Acids can be corrosive, and chemical fumes can be harmful when inhaled. Industrial hygiene and safety specialists take all the proper precautions and see that employees wear the right protective equipment.

They must know the properties of each chemical used, and how it reacts when mixed with other substances or when exposed to the atmosphere.

They also check noise levels to make sure they do not get above levels that might prove harmful to humans. They constantly monitor dust levels and fumes and gases, making certain they are well within safety limits.

They must be thoroughly familiar with the operation of every phase of the chemical plant, and have the insight to correct any potential difficulties.

All large chemical companies now have staffs of industrial hygienists and safety engineers. Smaller companies without full-time staffs either use part-time specialists or consultants. Many federal and state government agencies also employ experts in these fields to write safety and health standards, and see that they are enforced by inspecting plants. Two of the most active federal agencies in this area are the Occupational Safety and Health Administration (OSHA) and the Environmental Protection Agency (EPA).

One of the chief benefits of a job as an industrial hygienist or safety engineer, in addition to salary, which is roughly equal to that of other chemical engineers, is the opportunity to see and understand all types of plant operations. This provides a broad general background of knowledge and skill that is useful in advancing to higher career positions.

A bachelor's degree in chemistry or chemical engineering is needed for this fast-developing career field. Some new master's degree programs have been started, and on-the-job training is available.

[45]

INFORMATION SPECIALISTS

There are several career fields open in the general area of information, writing, and library science. Chemical librarians, for example, work for universities, government, institutes, and industry. Chemical companies maintain excellent technical libraries. Librarians use computer services to help researchers find needed information in technical reports and documents. Similarly, information chemists search technical and trade records, documents and patents to supply scientists, chemists, and administrators with the data required to make important management and technical decisions.

Some information chemists become terminology specialists. They develop new technical vocabularies and control reference systems for product information, which supplies experts with the data necessary to make critical decisions.

Science information services are related to library services. Sometimes the two are separate, but more often they are not. People in information services are concerned with storing, retrieving, and channeling material to the proper people. They almost always use computers in their work.

The line between chemical librarians and information specialists is fast being erased. Because computers are now being used nearly everywhere for information storage and retrieval, most chemical librarians today—and all of them in the future—need to be skilled in the use of information science.

Another field is chemical science writing. Writers and editors prepare technical manuals, public information releases, university, institute, government, or company newspapers, sales brochures, fact sheets, and film scripts.

**Chemical librarians must see that their libraries
are well-stocked with up-to-date technical literature.**

Chemical writers and editors should have a flair for writing, some journalistic training, and a bachelor's degree in chemistry. Salaries are generally considerably higher than those for reporters or writers on newspapers or in other nontechnical jobs.

Information scientists should have a degree or degrees in chemistry ranging up to a Ph.D. Additionally, they should have training or experience in computer operation, languages, and technical writing. Because of the extra educational requirements, the pay for these specialists is higher than for chemical writers or librarians.

Chemical librarians usually have a bachelor's degree in chemistry and a master's degree in library science. More and more of them have advanced training in information science. Salaries are good compared with those of other career librarians, and in some cases are better than the salaries of chemists with B.S. degrees who work in laboratories.

PATENT LAWYERS

Patent law is a challenging career for lawyers with a chemical background. Patents are issued by the U.S. Government to individuals and to companies to protect new inventions, products or processes, from being copied, stolen, or used by others. Patents are granted exclusively for a period of seventeen years.

Most inventors sell or lease patent rights for their inventions to a company that has the money and facilities to produce and market the product. Patents can also be licensed to other individuals or companies. Lawyers advise their clients on these matters.

When a new product or process is developed, patent lawyers search the records to establish the originality of the claim. If it is original, they file for the patent, and they negotiate agreements between the inventor and those who are interested in buying or leasing the patented product.

Patents are very important in the chemical business, because if there were no means by which companies could protect new inventions, they could not support the large research programs necessary to test and develop space-age technologies, new medicines and drugs, better chemical processing methods, or other essential consumer products.

Some chemists become patent agents and patent examiners through on-the-job training. Patent agents represent clients who desire patents on their inventions to be registered with the U.S. Patent Office. Patent examiners, who work for the government, have the power to reject or allow patent applications.

A law degree is required for patent attorneys. Most patent attorneys working in the chemical industry have at least a bachelor's degree in chemistry or a closely related field, plus a law degree. Because of the specialized technical knowledge required, plus the legal training and education, patent attorneys are paid excellent salaries.

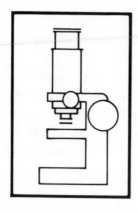

Chemistry:
A Career for You?

How do you know if you want to pursue a career in chemistry or engineering? Discuss it with your teachers and counselors. Talk with people in the chemistry and chemical engineering departments at nearby colleges and universities. Mix with the students. Write to companies, government agencies, and associations for brochures and other literature that describe career fields.

To prepare for jobs as chemists and chemical engineers, you should start early in high school. First, the importance of mathematics cannot be overestimated. A good, broad-based math foundation in high school is necessary to prepare for college-level work, such as analytical geometry and calculus. This normally involves four years of college-preparatory math in high school.

But even if you are not sure of future plans, math courses are a good bet because they are important subjects in preparing for all branches of science and engineering, and for many nontechnical fields as well.

You should also take biology, physics, and, of course, chemistry. The American Chemical Society (ACS) recommends that high school students take at least two, and preferably three or four, years of a foreign language—German, French, or Russian. The ACS also says a strong training in written and spoken English is desirable, four years if possible, as well as two or three years study in the social sciences.

In college, the courses a chemistry major takes vary from one campus to another. However, at most schools, the first two years include two or three specialized courses in science and mathematics, and several general courses, such as history, English, foreign language, political science, and economics.

At most colleges and universities, the introductory course in general chemistry, including qualitative and elementary quantitative analysis, is followed by organic chemistry. A course in physical chemistry based on calculus and college physics occurs no later than the junior year, and is followed by a course in advanced analytical chemistry.

Generally, students have the opportunity to choose advanced courses in specialized fields of chemistry, such as biochemistry, inorganic chemistry, and independent study.

While such a sequence of courses may seem formidable, remember that each course builds on a previous one. Successful career preparation in college, as well as in high school, involves mastering new knowledge and skills, step by step.

The American Chemical Society, the American Institute of Chemical Engineers, and other organizations say that there is no "best college or university" for chemistry majors. In fact, in one private survey it was found that 2,400 technically trained people employed by one large chemical company were educated at 258 different colleges and universities.

Most career professionals agree that dedicated students can gain good training in chemistry at almost any recognized college or university. The American Chemical Society does have a list of approved schools, which may be helpful to your planning. The main key to your collegiate success, however, will depend on your own initiative and dedication to hard work.

HOW MUCH EDUCATION?

How much college is required, and are advanced degrees necessary? As we have seen in the preceding chapters, there are jobs for all kinds of chemists in almost every chemistry-related industry. High school chemistry is sufficient for some chemical assistant and technician jobs. An associate's degree in chemical technology from a two-year college is required for other technician jobs.

For a position as a professional chemist or as a chemical engineer, however, at least four years of college and a bachelor's degree are necessary. For those interested in careers in research, or as teachers or professors in colleges and universities, further education is suggested. Another year or so is usually required for a master's degree, and from three to five years for a Ph.D. Also, because of the increasing complexity of modern technology, many career-minded students seek additional degrees in chemistry, chemical engineering, or business administration.

While studying for a college degree, many students find part-time work in their school's chemistry department. This in itself is educational. Students working toward advanced degrees can often obtain assistantships or fellowships.

The National Science Foundation supports teacher education and research. During summers, one can attend intensive short courses, take regular courses, or work with an academic research scientist.

Industrial and governmental chemists also have opportunities for continuing education. They may attend in-house courses, intensive short courses, and evening classes. Frequently, tuition is paid by the employer.

JOB HUNTING

After graduation—be it high school, technical school, or college—there are many ways to seek a job in the chemical industry. One excellent method is to explore the employment opportunities listed with school or college placement offices. Another is to contact any of the companies, institutions, government agencies, or schools and universities that employ chemists and chemical engineers. Information about jobs may also be obtained through such professional associations as the American Chemical Society and the American Institute of Chemical Engineers.

Job demands for chemists and chemical engineers vary from year to year, and depend upon economic conditions, the number of applicants versus number of job openings, and other factors. However, the American Chemical Society says, "chemists seem to fare as well as most other workers when seeking employment in times of both prosperity and recession."

And the American Institute of Chemical Engineers says, "most chemical companies report shortages of chemical engineers. There seems to be every indication at this time that the shortage will become even more critical in the early 1980s. Chemical engineering is a dynamic field and could offer many opportunities for employment when you enter the job market."

Salaries vary greatly, according to employer, job classification, and chemical specialty. According to a 1976 American Chemical Society survey, the median an-

nual salary for a chemist with a bachelor's degree and one year's experience or less was $11,000. This ranged from a low of $8,400 to a high of $14,000. For chemists with a master's degree and a year or less experience, the median annual salary was $13,000, and for chemists with a doctor's degree and the same amount of experience, the median was $17,700.

In another survey taken in 1976 of all chemists, those in industry made the highest salaries and those in education ranked lowest. Industrial chemists with several years experience averaged $20,000 per year. Chemists working for government agencies were next, averaging $19,700 annually. Those working for nonprofit organizations such as private institutions and foundations made an average $16,000 a year, and chemistry teachers had a median annual salary of $11,300.

By specific job classification, chemists who had advanced to the ranks of management were found to make the most money, a median annual salary of $26,000. Next, in order, were marketing and production, $18,800; research and development, $18,600; specialists, such as chemists in analysis, consulting, writing, and programming, $16,500; and teaching, again, $11,300.

Unfortunately, female chemists for the most part are still being paid from several hundred to a few thousand dollars per year less than their male counterparts, according to surveys. However, much effort has been focused on correcting this situation in recent years, and today, many starting chemists and chemical engineers are being paid strictly according to their qualifications

Efforts are being made to have the salaries of female chemists equal to those of male chemists.

and capabilities, not in relation to their sex, color, creed, or religion.

As a general rule of thumb, chemical engineers make 10 to 20 percent more a year than chemists in most job categories. This is in part because more chemical engineers by percentage work for industrial chemical companies than do chemists, and these companies generally pay more than government, institutions, or colleges and universities.

Overall, the salaries of all chemists and chemical engineers—both starting out and in mid-career—average higher than in most other professions. The same is true, for the most part, for chemical technicians, laboratory personnel, and production, maintenance and utility workers, and others in chemical jobs that do not require college degrees.

For example, in one nationwide survey taken in 1975, the average hourly wage of all production workers in manufacturing was $4.81. The average for production workers in chemical and allied products was $5.37, and for industrial chemical production workers, it was $5.93. The average hourly wage for production people involved with petroleum and coal products was $6.42.

OTHER BENEFITS

In addition to better-than-average salaries in most jobs, the chemical industry, government agencies, schools and universities, and private institutions and research centers involved in chemical work offer excellent benefits packages for employees. While these packages differ somewhat from company to company, or from agency to institution, they generally include the following:

—Life and comprehensive health insurance at no cost, or at greatly reduced rates.

—Liberal disability benefits and sick pay for employees unable to work due to sickness or accident.

—Paid holidays and vacation. New employees usually get two weeks paid vacation, with extra time after working a certain number of years.

—Retirement programs that provide company-paid, or company- and employee-paid pension funds after the employee works a certain number of years, and/or reaches a certain age.

—Many companies have stock option plans whereby employees may buy stock in their company at reduced rates.

—Most companies, schools, institutions, and government agencies have continuing education programs where employees may further their studies with costs paid for in part or in full by their employers.

Aside from salary and benefit packages, many people in the chemical career field find that some of their most meaningful rewards are ones that cannot directly be measured in dollars and cents.

They find pride and excitement in discovering and developing the products and processes that help feed, shelter, and clothe people, and that help prolong life and improve living conditions. They enjoy career satisfaction in applying their knowledge and experience to the ever-present challenges that jobs in the chemical industry offer. And they know that because of the variety of opportunities available in this progressive profession, that their individual growth and advancement will be limited only by their own desire, talent, and dedication.

Additional Sources of Information

The American Chemical Society
Department of Educational Activities
1155 16th Street, N.W.
Washington, D.C. 20036

The American Institute of Chemical Engineers
345 East 47th Street
New York, New York 10017

American Society of Biological Chemists
9650 Rockville Pike
Bethesda, Maryland 20014

Bureau of Mines
Washington, D.C. 20240

Canadian Society for Chemical Engineering
Suite 906
151 Slater Street
Ottawa, Ontario K1P 5H3

Chemical Institute of Canada
Suite 906
151 Slater Street
Ottawa, Ontario K1P 5H3

The Manufacturing Chemists
Association
1825 Connecticut Avenue, N.W.
Washington, D.C. 20009

National Association of Trade and
Technical Schools
2021 L Street, N.W.
Washington, D.C. 20036

National Council of Technical Schools
1835 K Street, N.W.
Washington, D.C. 20006

National Science Teachers
Association
1742 Connecticut Avenue, N.W.
Washington, D.C. 20009

Occupational Safety and
Health Administration
14th and Constitution, N.W.
Washington, D.C. 20210

Scientific Manpower Commission
1776 Massachusetts Avenue, N.W.
Washington, D.C. 20036

Society of Mining Engineers
of the American Institute of
Mining, Metallurgical, and
Petroleum Engineers
540 Arapeen Drive
Research Park
Salt Lake City, Utah 84108

U.S. Civil Service Commission
1900 E Street, N.W.
Washington, D.C. 20415

U.S. Department of Agriculture
Washington, D.C. 20250

U.S. Department of Health, Education
and Welfare
Office of Education
Division of Higher Education
  and/or
Division of Vocational and Technical
  Education
Washington, D.C. 20202

U.S. Government Printing Office
Superintendent of Documents
Washington, D.C. 20402

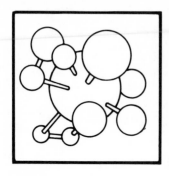

Further Reading

The following books or pamphlets can be ordered for additional information on careers in chemistry:

American Chemical Society List of Approved Schools, American Chemical Society

Careers in Chemistry: Questions and Answers, American Chemical Society

Careers in Chemistry Today, American Chemical Society

Federal Career Directory 1975: A Guide for College Students, U. S. Government Printing Office

Guide to Federal Career Literature, U.S. Government Printing Office

Keys to Careers in Science and Technology, National Science Teachers Association

Occupational Outlook Handbook, U.S. Government Printing Office

Professional Women and Minorities: A Manpower Data Resource Service, Scientific Manpower Commission

Professionals in Chemistry, American Chemical Society

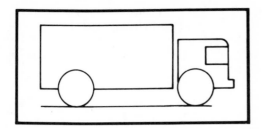

Index

Information specialists, 46
Inorganic chemists, 5
Inventions, protection of, 48–49

Kettering, Charles F., 7

Lawyers, patent, 48–49
Librarians, chemical, 46

Manufacturing Chemists Association, 59
Market research, opportunities in, 37–38
Medicine and chemistry, 3

National Association of Trade and Technical Schools, 59
National Council of Technical Schools, 59
National Science Foundation, 39, 52
National Science Teachers Foundation, 59
Nuclear energy, 3

Occupational Safety and Health Administration (OSHA), 45, 59
Organic chemistry, 4–5

Patent lawyers, 48–49
Petroleum industry, 3, 9
Pharmaceuticals, 3, 9
Physical chemist, 5
Pilot plants, 16–18
Plants
    maintenance of, 27–28
    pilot, 16–18
    production, 21–25
Production, careers in, distribution and traffic, 29–31
    industrial service, 28–29
    maintenance of plants, 27–28
    production engineers, 21–23, 25

quality control, 23–24
technicians, 24–25

Quality control, chemists in, 23–24

Research
    applied, 9–11
    basic, 8
    careers in, 4, 7–15
    education requirements, 13–14
    in large colleges and universities, 40–42
    opportunities, 12–14
    personal qualities, 11–12
    rewards of, 14–15
    U.S. government grants to, 40

Safety engineers, 44–45
Sales, opportunities in, 32–37
Scientific Manpower Commission, 59
Society of Mining Engineers of the American Institute of Mining, Metallurgical, and Petroleum Engineers, 59

Teaching chemistry as a career, 4–5, 39–40
Textile industry and chemistry, 3

U.S. Bureau of Mines, 58
U.S. Civil Service Commission, 59
U.S. Department of Agriculture, 12, 59
U.S. Department of Health, Education, and Welfare, 59
U.S. Government Printing Office, 59
U.S. Patent Office, 48–49
U.S. Public Health Service, 12

Writers, chemical, 48

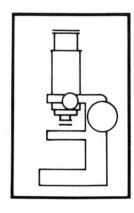

About the Author

L.B. Taylor, Jr. knows the chemical industry well, for he works within it. After graduating from Florida State University, Mr. Taylor began his career in the aerospace industry, spending ten years at Cape Kennedy and the Kennedy Space Center in Florida. He then joined the chemical field.

L.B. Taylor's writing abilities have served him well. He is the author of six books and more than 200 magazine articles. When not at his typewriter in Williamsburg, Virginia, Mr. Taylor travels extensively.